Choose Life
Not Death

Nakeisha Creighton

Nakeisha Creighton

Scripture quotations noted NKJV are taken from the New King James Version® Foundation Study Bible, copyright © 1982 by Thomas Nelson. Used by permission. All rights reserved.

Scripture quotations noted NLT are taken from the Holy Bible, New Living Translation, copyright © 1996, 2004, 2007 by Tyndale House Foundation. Used by permission. All rights reserved.

Table of Content

Acknowledgement

Giving honor to God the Father, Jesus the Son and the Holy Spirit who is the head of my life. I thank God for my (G.T.O.F) God's Temple of Faith Ministries family, my very own Bishop Leroy McClain Sr. and his wife/Co-pastor Pamela McClain for being obedient to the call of God. I pray for a continuing outpouring of God's spirit upon you both, and many abundant blessings for you and your family. I am grateful for the phenomenal teaching I receive at G.T.O.F. Ministries. I thank God for my two blessed, beautiful, and amazing children, Shaniyla and Dario. I thank God for my parents, (my dad) Michael Mitchell and (my mother) Leitha Creighton who was called home on July 29, 2007. I just thank God for all of my family and friends. God bless you all.

Introduction

This book is inspired by the urgency I received from the Holy Spirit on the night of July 25, 2019. That Thursday evening, I was on a conference call for prayer with two of my sisters in Christ, and after we finished praying, we remained on the phone a little longer to encourage one another. One of my sister's being unctioned by the Holy Spirit spoke about the 2019 USA Prophetic Convention our Bishop and Co-Pastor attended. She told us she watched it on YouTube; she encouraged us to watch it. As she spoke about what she had watched, she got excited. She filled us in about a subject the man of God "Prophet Sadhu Sundar Selvaraj" spoke about where He was informing people about the importance of prayer with their families every night for at least an hour before bed. After being encouraged, I prayed and spoke with my children about God for an hour that night before going to bed. That night, as I fell asleep, I had a powerful encounter with God. He gave me this exceptional idea to share what I knew about Jesus with people through this book. God wants all people to discover the truth about who Jesus is and what He has done for all of us on the cross and after He has risen. I wrote all that he shared with me during that encounter. I am so excited that God chose me to carry out this mission. I pray that everyone who reads this book will accept Jesus as his/her Lord and Savior and begin a new relationship with God through Jesus today.

Nakeisha Creighton

CHAPTER ONE
God's Saving Grace

I want to give you a little background about me because I believe many can identify with my story and I know that it is only by God's grace I am here today. I was born in Brooklyn, N.Y. and lived on Howard Ave along with my mom and sisters. I grew up in what most would call a dysfunctional family. I am the second oldest from the seven beautiful daughters my mother the late Leitha Creighton has given birth to. At an early age, I have experienced many things that have caused fear, bitterness, hurt, and brokenness. At age 5, I remember my mother would lock herself in the bathroom for hours to smoke or get high, because of her addiction to crack cocaine Meanwhile, my sister's and I would scramble for food each day. By the age of 6, my mother met this man who battled with an addiction to crack cocaine. I can remember the many times they would close themselves in the room and smoke together and after several hours things would get physical between the two of them. It was not long before he was living with us, and the molestation began. My mother trusted him to bathe us and it was during those times he would molest my sisters and I. One day when he was bathing one of my little sisters, I opened the bathroom door without knocking to tell him something as I opened the door, I saw him rubbing and touching my sister inappropriately. He glared at me and with a firm tone in his voice and said: "close the door now." I was so angry because of what he was doing to my helpless little sister. Although he would do the same thing to me, I was more upset because I felt as a big sister my job was to protect her, but I was not able too. I wanted to tell my mother, but I was too afraid. As the days passed by, I was hoping for things to change, but because of my mother's dependency on drugs, she stopped worrying about what or how we felt, ate or were doing most of the time. One day after going through half of the day with no food and hearing my sister's crying and complaining about how hungry they were, I decided I would run across the street to the grocery store and steal food for us to eat. This idea had become an everyday occurrence for me until one day the owner of the store caught me. He said, "Hey, what are you doing?" I just looked at him with the items in my hand. He then said just don't come back in here. I thought to myself, oh there goes our food. We went to bed hungry some nights because my mom did not have food in the house. As I continued to hope for brighter days one day after walking home from school with my big sister as we walked into the house there were police everywhere. We were all scared, but the police assured us we would be ok. One police told us to come with him, so we followed him into the police car. We were crying because we wanted our mom to come with us. After we arrived at the police precinct. The police asked us were we hungry, and we all said "yes". He gave us all peanut butter and jelly sandwiches. While we were eating our sandwiches, I overheard the police say to another police they took us because our neighbors called CPS (Child Protective Services) on our mother. Later that evening they placed us in a foster home in Brownsville. My sisters and I lacked home training and discipline because our mom did not teach us much about how you were to conduct yourself outside or anywhere. We got beaten often because of this. My sisters and I moved to several foster homes, this was mainly from the foster parent becoming frustrated or overwhelmed with having to teach and train us. By the age of 12, we were separated and sent to two different homes. They split us up between two foster homes. They sent my 5 little sisters to one home and my older sister and I went to another. This was so devastating because I wanted us to be together, but no foster parent wanted to take 7 girls. The home my older sister and I moved to, we experienced a lot of verbal and physical abuse. My oldest sister had a physical fight with our foster-mother daughter one day, and she was thrown out and sent to another home. I became very depressed because I missed my sister and I was being abused with no one to talk to about it. Eventually, after learning how to travel on the bus and train, I grew the courage to run away. At 18, I signed myself out of foster care where I could grow a close bond with my mother being that she was 6 years clean from crack cocaine. I found out my dad's whereabouts, and I asked my mom about his absence throughout my younger years. She told me that my dad was in and out of prison most of my younger life and he had just come home and if I wanted to meet him I could. After meeting my dad and still feeling empty inside, I moved on and tried to find love in the men I dated to overcome the pain I often felt. I would get into many verbally, emotionally, and physically abusive relationships thinking I deserved everything I got. I had low self-esteem to where I hated and rejected myself, especially because I did not feel loved by anyone. By the age of 21 I had my first child, a baby girl, a month after the birth of my daughter, my mother died. Approximately 4 months after my mother's death, I became homeless and went into a shelter where I spent 8 months. then I got an apartment in the Bronx. I landed a superb job as a genealogist, but I needed a babysitter, so I moved my daughter's father in with us. He was verbally and physically abusive, but I thought that was how he showed he loved me, so I dealt with the abuse for several years. One day after having a big fight with him, he threatened to not babysit our daughter for me to go to work as he had often done. I was tired of calling into work every time he decided he did not want to watch our daughter, so I grew the courage to kick him out. I then searched for a therapist to help me combat every lie I had partnered with. Some months after attending a few therapy sessions, I realized that it was not enough to heal the hurt, pain, or brokenness that was so deeply rooted inside of me. After several months I stopped attending therapy, and I jumped into another relationship where I shortly realized I needed healing from the previous relationship I was in. The man I had gotten into the relationship with was addicted to alcohol and cocaine, but I wanted to make the relationship work just to feel like someone loved me. I dragged all my brokenness into that relationship where I faced more verbal and physical abuse. I had become depressed and shattered because the man I was in relations with had a profoundly serious addiction to alcohol and cocaine. Although I did not like his addictions, I would drink with him to drown out my feelings. About a year later we moved in together, thinking we could help each other, but I became drained most of the time trying to help him, plus I still had to take care of my daughter. I then became pregnant with our son and after giving birth to him I realized I was not the best mother to my daughter, so I felt this was a second chance to change that. I became homeless again but this time we were homeless for 2 years after moving from shelter to shelter and sometimes sleeping in our vehicle I just wanted all the chaos to end. I needed help, so I reached out to my dad. I reached out to my dad because I felt this would be a second chance for him as a grandfather since he did not raise me. My dad and girlfriend agreed to help me. He told me we just had to move to Syracuse N.Y. where they were living. I was so excited thinking to myself that this would be a great fresh start for the children and I. We moved in with my dad and his girlfriend about a month later. A week after moving in with my dad; he told me we needed to go into a shelter because there was not enough room for us, so the kids and I went into the shelter. We moved into an apartment after a month of being there. After moving into our apartment and getting situated, I moved my son's father in with me, even though I knew he was still struggling with his addiction to alcohol and cocaine. I moved him in with us because a part of me felt I could not raise my son by myself and I was afraid of being alone.

It was not long after moving him in with us that the physical and verbal abuse started up between us. I started looking for a job so I could be out of the house more often. I landed a seasonal job at a call center which lasted for several months then I became a school Bus Driver. Every day I went to work smiling on the outside but internally I was hurting, broken, and felt defeated. One day while I was at work, I met this woman whom God sent to help me. The woman would always smile and speak to me. After several months she started asking me if I wanted to come with her to her church. I knew I needed help, but I would still say "no, I'm ok". One day my son's father and I had a big fight because he crashed my car while heading to pick up our son from school. I remember crying and thinking to myself everything I work hard for he destroys. I had reached my breaking point, and I had enough of my life and all that it consisted of. I wanted a change in my life so I reached out to the women from my job at the time and I asked her if I could come to church with her. She said "yes" and that weekend I went with her to church and met this powerful, loving, and caring woman of God who greeted me with the love I so desperately needed. The very first day I was there, I knew that was where I needed to be. After attending that church for several weeks, they invited me to go to a conference with them and while attending the conference the woman of God did an altar call for anyone who wanted to surrender their life to Jesus. As I heard the altar call, I can remember being pushed to the front by the Holy Spirit where I had given my life to Jesus. Today I am redeemed through the precious blood of my Lord and Savior Jesus Christ. **"In Him, we have redemption through His blood, the forgiveness of sins, according to the riches of His grace" Ephesians 1; 7 NKJV.**

Nakeisha Creighton

CHAPTER TWO

Step into the Knowing

Let me ask you a question. Do you know where you will spend eternity after transitioning from this earth? I want you to think about this question because it is very important that you can answer it with confidence and assurance. I know that people will not spend too much time pondering on this question because it can cause one to become fearful, especially if they are not sure. I have asked this question to many people who have answered with certainty while others just did not have an answer. Well, allow me to help you with your answer. We all have an appointment with death and will spend eternity in Heaven or Hell one day. Some people that have answered this question with certainty were very sarcastic in their response. Their response would sound like "YES HEAVEN" with a look on their face as if they are thinking "Didn't you know that"? I would then reply, "What makes you so sure of your answer"? They would answer "I am kind" or "I am a friendly person." The Holy Spirit would then tell me to inform them of His truth. I would then say, "although those characteristics are great to have, those characteristics alone will not get you into heaven. There is only one way to heaven, and that's through Jesus Christ." We find this in God's word in the book of John **Chapter 14 Verse 6 NKJV "Jesus said to him, "I am the way, the truth, and the life. No one comes to the Father except through Me"**. Jesus is the only way to God the Father, the true God in heaven. Jesus is the channel of resurrection/ new life to us. When I would share God's truth people did not want to believe instead, they would reject it. I realize that many people have heard of Jesus or have heard people speak about Him, but they have never experienced Him for themselves. I can remember at the beginning of my walk with God through Jesus I would hear people referring to God as their provider and sometimes I repeated it around other believers. I would say "yes God is my provider" and deep down I didn't believe that. Have you ever said something just so you could fit in and feel you are a part of something or someone? Well, you are not alone because that was me! I didn't believe that God was my provider because I had not experienced Him in that way. I believe that you cannot believe in something fully until you experience it for yourself. If I told you that Chipotle tastes good, but you never tasted it for yourself to know if it is good or not, you most likely will not agree with me. At the beginning of my walk with God, I believed that He existed, but I denied His power of all that He is capable of because I was too afraid to let go of my way of doing things. I was so used to doing things my way, for example, I relied on my paycheck instead of God, I trusted gambling to win money which became an addiction for me instead of relying on God's help with my bills. Over time, because of the gambling addiction, my life became a complete disaster. I ended up losing my car because it got repoed, I was facing an eviction and on the verge of being kicked out of my apartment, and I was losing my children because they no longer trust me. Most people I know that have battled with an addiction have made promises that they were not capable of keeping. This had become the story of my life; I would make promises to my children that I just could not fulfill. I remember this one particular day my daughter stood before me with tears running down her face and said "mom you always promise me stuff and you never get it" I instantly felt bad. Shame and guilt had overwhelmed me because I knew I wanted to change, but it just wasn't as easy as it sounds. I was in a battle in my mind, one part of me wanted to change, but the addiction was a stronghold that was also tugging on me. That day, after going into my room and crying, I came up with a plan to find a therapist to help me. I wanted to change so bad I began going to see a therapist that same week. After attending the therapy sessions twice, a week and following the plans which he had put into place for me to follow for me to overcome the addiction. Some of his plans consisted of: cutting up all casino cards and vowing to never go to the casino again, but I would still sneak to the casino to gamble. I want to point out something to you before I continue. Did you notice that during that time? I was a born-again believer. I had accepted Jesus as my Lord and Savior. I was attending church regularly, but; I was still struggling with addiction. It was not long before I realized that the therapist could not help me remove the addiction that was driving me to run and gamble each time I got paid. During the fourth therapy session I heard a voice speak to me and say, "Why are you there?" I looked around the room, but I knew deep inside that this was the Holy Spirit speaking to me. I immediately got a revelation that a therapist is just a person in a fleshly body like you and I. They're trained to sit and talk to people, they're trained to give people advice, and they're trained to give people strategies of what they believe would work. I want to let you that God is the real (physician, healer, deliverer, helper, strong tower, protector, provider). That therapist may have been wrestling with his own giants or strongholds. He needed a Savior (Jesus) just like you and I. That day I knew that I was not going back to another therapy session. I am not telling you this so you can stop going to see a therapist if you feel you need too or for you to never consider therapy. I am just sharing my story of what God had done for me. I left that day not knowing that God was about to deliver me from gambling forever. That night after returning home from gambling and feeling down because I spent all my money. I went into my room and dropped to my knees, not having a clue of how I should pray or what I should pray. I remember saying "God if you are who everyone says you are then, show me by removing this gambling addiction, I don't want to be like this anymore, help me pay my bills, and help my children to trust me again." I want to tell you that God delivered me that day. God does not want you to pretend when talking to Him. He wants you to come to Him just the way you are with all your addictions, anger, foul mouth, and whatever else you are struggling with. I did not notice right away but after two weeks of not having the urge to want to go gamble, I was standing in my living room and I thought "wow I have not gone to the casino for two weeks now and I don't even have an urge to go." I started leaping for joy while praising God and screaming "Thank you Lord you heard and answered me." God delivered me from the gambling addiction, and He blessed my children and I with a car, and I did not get evicted because He provided the money for my rent. When God delivers you, there will be no residue. Since then God has been my provider and has helped me every step of the way. When we get out of the way and allow God to assist us, we can experience the true character of who God truly is. God wants to provide for you, protect you, comfort you, be there for you every step of the way. I believe God chose me to author this book because He wants you to know Him as your provider.

CHAPTER THREE
Truth

God wants you to know the truth about His love for you. Let me share a story with you about the beginning of my walk with Christ before I had a true understanding of God's love. I remember months after giving my life to Jesus and continuing to attend this church I was going to weekly. I can remember going to church every week but not knowing why I wanted to know Jesus or if I even had the proper view of who He is. I would go to church and just stare at the congregation of people. I didn't even know why I was going anymore. Come on, I know you have done that before. I thought my job was to judge the members of the congregation. I can remember questions or statements I would make to myself, some that would go as such 'Why are these people shouting and getting excited whenever the pastor speaks about Jesus?' or "I think these people are just acting"! I realized that the thoughts I had about those people were all wrong. I found out that those people had something that I did not have. They had a relationship with Jesus. I had yet to experience Jesus for myself because I was just going to church to keep busy and to keep my mind from the chaos back at home. Over time, because of my lack of relationship and understanding of Jesus, I came to church Sunday after Sunday with the same thoughts swimming around in my mind. I thought I knew what being a believer was all about. I was convinced that if I just came to church and did good and was kind to people, I would surely go to heaven. Sadly many people believe that they would be rewarded after death if they do more good than bad or if they pay tithes and go to church, especially because some are taught this false hope which isn't found in the word of God.

Billy Graham, an American Evangelist, once said, "Our salvation doesn't depend on us and our good works! If it did, no one would ever go to heaven because God's standard is nothing less than perfection. God is holy, and even one sin— just one—would be enough to keep you out of heaven. The bible says, For whoever keeps the whole law and yet stumbles at just one point is guilty of breaking all of it (James 2:10)" It took me some time to receive this revelation. I remember trying to do kind things and or trying to be nice to people that were not always nice or kind to me and it was a struggle. Did you hear me say that I would try, I said try because I would be kind one minute and flying off the handle the next. I felt very unstable. I felt like a ticking time bomb waiting to explode. After some much-needed time spent with God through Jesus, it was with His help I was healed from that behavior. I also realized that I was not capable of being kind to people who were not always so kind back without God's help. If this is how you feel I encourage you to ask God for His help and let Him guide you. You are not alone. Many people struggle in this area. In the book of **Romans Chapter 7 Verse 18 NKJV it reads "For I know that in me (that is, in my flesh) nothing good dwells; for to will is present with me, but *how to perform what is good I do not find*"**. The writer Paul an apostle was born in Tarsus, the capital city of the Roman province of Cilicia, in southeast Asia minor. He was a strict Pharisee. We first find him in Jerusalem during the death of the Christian martyr Stephen. Paul was known as Saul before his Christian conversion after meeting Jesus on a road in Damascus. In the verse, we just read Paul said that he knows that nothing good lives in him (because of the evil that lives in man's heart Genesis 6; 5) or his flesh and even though he has a willingness to do good, he cannot do good on his own without the help or assistance of Jesus. When I first read that scripture, I thought this is the reality of our human sinful nature. When you try to do things in your strength, you will fail! God is the only one who can change our deep rebellion against Him and His ways. Therefore God the Father in heaven sent His son Jesus as a sacrifice to pay the price for you and my sins, which we will speak more about in a later chapter.

Nakeisha Creighton

CHAPTER FOUR

Man's Relationship with God Broken

What is sin? Sin is a condition in which the heart is corrupted and inclined toward evil; rebellion against God; wrongdoing or transgression of God's law. Here are some examples of our behavior, our thoughts, or things we say or do because of sin: disobeying God, dishonoring our parents, murder, anger, gossip, lust, idolatry, lying, and many more. Sin, regardless of how serious it is, always has an effect which is separation. Sin separates us from God. This separation from God is death. Whether the sin that is caused harms us or someone else, all sin is against God because He is holy. In the book of **Isaiah Chapter 59 Verse 2 NKJV it reads, "But your iniquities have separated you from your God; And your sins have hidden His face from you So that He will not hear"**. Isaiah, the son of Amoz often referred to as a prophet of God whom He sent His messages through, called to prophesy. In the verse we read Isaiah was speaking about the iniquities that have separated the people from God. As a result, they will not enjoy any personal communion with God because of the evil in their lives, and the prayers put up to God will be denied an answer. God loves us all, even when we have sinned, but He will not reward us for sinning. Next, we will learn how and when sin first entered the world, let us read in the book of **Genesis Chapter 2 verses 7-9 NKJV And the Lord God formed man of the dust of the ground, and breathed into his nostrils the breath of life; and man became a living being. The Lord God planted a garden eastward in Eden, and there He put the man whom He had formed. And out of the ground the Lord God made every tree grow that is pleasant to the sight and good for food. The tree of life was**

also in the midst of the garden, and the tree of the knowledge of good and evil. God created the man from the element of the earth (dust). Then God breathed into his nostrils. The word for breath in Hebrew is ruach. Ruach is the same word for Spirit or wind, as in both ancient Greek (pneuma) and Latin (spiritus). God created the man by putting His breath, His Spirit, within him. He made the man of both: an earthly, and of heavenly matter. The man became a living being. Only man is a living being made in the image of God according to the Word of God in **Genesis 1:26 "So God created man in His own image; in the image of God He created him; male and female He created them."** God specifically planted the Garden of Eden; it was a place God made to be a perfect habitation for Adam (and later, Eve). Then God made trees out of the ground good for food. As we skip down a few verses in the book of **Genesis 2:15-19 NKJV "Then the Lord God took the man and put him in the garden of Eden to tend and keep it. And the Lord God commanded the man, saying, "Of every tree of the garden you may freely eat; but of the tree of the knowledge of good and evil you shall not eat, for in the day that you eat of it you shall surely die." And the Lord God said, "It is not good that man should be alone; I will make him a helper comparable to him." Out of the ground the Lord God formed every beast of the field and every bird of the air, and brought them to Adam to see what he would call them. And whatever Adam called each living creature, that was its name".** Adam tended and kept the Garden of Eden. God commanded Adam two separate commandments here, a positive and a negative commandment. It spelled the positive commandment out in the words "Of every tree of the garden you may freely eat." It contained the negative commandment in the words" but of the tree of the knowledge of good and evil you shall not eat" (verse 17). When God said "for in the day that you eat of it you shall surely die" God was not referring to the man dropping dead on an instant but, of the human body aging followed by a physical death and immediate spiritual death (separation from God). It was not God's intention for the man to remain alone, seeing that all other creatures were created in pairs, male and female specimens to enable them to "mate" and to reproduce their kind. In verse 19 we see that the man has a name, Adam, which means "ground" because God formed Adam out of the very element of the earth. God gave Adam authority over all the creatures. Adam named them under the special qualities each animal possessed. Let's skip down and continue in **Genesis Chapter 2 Verses 21-25 NK JV, "And the Lord God caused a deep sleep to fall on Adam, and he slept; and He took one of his ribs, and closed up the flesh in its place. Then the rib which the Lord God had taken from man He made into a woman, and He brought her to the man. And Adam said:**

"This is now bone of my bones

And flesh of my flesh;

She shall be called Woman,

Because she was taken out of Man."

Therefore a man shall leave his father and mother and be joined to his wife, and they shall become one flesh. And they were both naked, the man and his wife, and were not ashamed". God caused a deep sleep to fall upon Adam so that the surgery (this is the first surgery recorded in history) He performed on him would not cause him any pain. God made him unconscious while He took one of his ribs to form the woman. This was to imply equality and mutual respect and to forever remind Adam of their essential oneness. Adam's partner was made of his own flesh! This was a onetime occurrence and would not repeat itself because from this time on instead of woman emanating from the man, the man would emanate from a woman's womb. Verse (24) speaks about a man leaving the home of his parents to acquire a wife compatible with him, and who is a suitable mate for him to live with permanently. We see in verse 25 that it refers to the man and woman being naked and not being ashamed this was because although Adam had been equipped with the knowledge to give names to all creatures, the evil inclination did not become an active principle in him until he disobeyed God by eating from the forbidden tree and as a result sin entered the world, so up to this point Adam was not aware of the difference between good and evil. God always wanted to have a relationship with us. We have previously read how humans came into existence now, let us read more to understand how God's beautiful world has become corrupt. We will skip ahead in the same book of **Genesis to Chapter 3 Verses 1-7 NKJV**, it reads **"Now the serpent was more cunning than any beast of the field which the Lord God had made. And he said to the woman, "Has God indeed said, 'You shall not eat of every tree of the garden'?" And the woman said to the serpent, "We may eat the fruit of the trees of the garden; but of the fruit of the tree which *is* in the midst of the garden, God has said, 'You shall not eat it, nor shall you touch it, lest you die. " Then the serpent said to the woman, "You will not surely die. For God knows that in the day you eat of it your eyes will be opened, and you will be like God, knowing good and evil." So when the woman saw that the tree *was* good for food, that it *was* pleasant to the eyes, and a tree desirable to make *one* wise, she took of its fruit and ate. She also gave to her husband with her, and he ate. Then the eyes of both of them were opened, and they knew that they *were* naked; and they sewed fig leaves together and made themselves** coverings". The Hebrew word for serpent or snake is nachash because of its hiss. The serpent is portrayed as a deceptive creature. The Bible identifies Satan with the serpent in the book of **Revelation Chapter 12 Verse 9 NKJV "So the great dragon was cast out, that serpent of old, called the Devil and Satan, who deceives the whole world; he was cast to the earth, and his angels were cast out with him"**. Satan slandered the motives of God, Satan used the serpent to tempt Eve by asking her a question first, then rebelling against God. When we look at verse 2, we see that Eve added to God's command while responding to the serpent adding **"nor shall you touch it"** God did not forbid touching of the tree, but only eating of its fruit. God's word tells us not to add to His word in **Proverbs 30; 6 "Do not add to His words, Lest He rebuke you, and you be found a liar."** When one adds a restriction to God's commandment, instead of improving it, one causes harm to it, making it less effective instead of more effective. Satan drew Eve into a discussion with him and planted the seed of doubt about God's Word, then he contradicts what God said. Eve saw that the tree **"was pleasant to the eyes"** in verse 6. This is the lust of the eyes. Satan uses this trap to get people to delight in fantasies in their thought life. Eve **"took of its fruit and ate."** This is the lust of the flesh. Satan wants us to please our desires with things like pleasure, food, revenge, and many more. Eve saw that the tree was "desirable to make one wise". This is the pride of life. Satan wants us to desire to be exalted, to develop an attitude of arrogance or pride. This was Satan's prideful sin. He had attempted to take God's place. I believe that Eve may have thought that the reason why God had forbidden the tree was that its fruit was not tasty, and the poison of the fruit would result in death to those who ate it. Now she had convinced herself that its fruit was sweet. Then we read that she gave some to her husband, Adam. As we move to verse 7 which says **"Then the eyes of both of them were opened"** this was referring to intelligence (the mind's eye) and not to actually see. Let us continue to read in **Genesis Chapter 3 Verses 8-24 NKJV "And they heard the sound of the Lord God walking in the garden in the cool of the day, and Adam and his wife hid themselves from the presence of the Lord God among the trees of the garden. Then the Lord God called to Adam and said to him, "Where *are* you?" So he said, "I heard Your voice in the garden, and I was afraid because I was naked; and I hid myself." And He said, "Who told you that you *were* naked? Have you eaten from the tree of which I commanded you that you should not eat?" Then the man said, "The woman whom You gave *to be* with me, she gave me of the tree, and I ate." And the Lord God said to the woman, "What *is* this you have done?" The woman said, "The serpent deceived me, and I ate."**

So the Lord God said to the serpent:

"Because you have done this,

You *are* cursed more than all cattle,

And more than every beast of the field;

On your belly you shall go,

And you shall eat dust

All the days of your life.

And I will put enmity

Between you and the woman,

And between your seed and her Seed;

He shall bruise your head,

And you shall bruise His heel."

To the woman He said:

"I will greatly multiply your sorrow and your conception;

In pain you shall bring forth children;

Your desire *shall be* for your husband,

And he shall rule over you."

Then to Adam He said, "Because you have heeded the voice of your wife, and have eaten from the tree of which I commanded you, saying, 'You shall not eat of it':

"Cursed *is* the ground for your sake;

In toil you shall eat *of* it

All the days of your life.

Both thorns and thistles it shall bring forth for you,

And you shall eat the herb of the field.

In the sweat of your face you shall eat bread

Till you return to the ground,

For out of it you were taken;

For dust you *are,*

And to dust you shall return."

And Adam called his wife's name Eve, because she was the mother of all living.

Also for Adam and his wife the Lord God made tunics of skin, and clothed them. Then the Lord God said, "Behold,

the man has become like one of Us, to know good and evil. And now, lest he put out his hand and take also of the tree of life, and eat, and live forever"— therefore the Lord God sent him out of the garden of Eden to till the ground from which he was taken. So, He drove out the man; and He placed cherubim at the east of the garden of Eden, and a flaming sword which turned every way, to guard the way to the tree of life". In verse 8 the first thing we notice is that the word walking is associated with God's voice "they heard the sound of the Lord God walking in the garden". When Adam and Eve would hear God call to them, they would run to God just as a child happy to see his or her parents. Sin caused Adam to be afraid of God's presence and afraid of God's voice. Then, God called Adam, God called Adam not because He did not know where Adam was but because He wanted Adam to confess what he had done, by saying "I have sinned," and repent in his heart. God wants the wicked to repent, so they will not perish. Next it said that "Adam told God that he was afraid because he was naked; so, he hid himself". So, God asked Adam, "Who told you that you *were* naked"? meaning What is so different now? Because Adam stood before God previously without feeling naked?" We see that right after the forbidden fruit was eaten, things changed immediately. The serpent was condemned from this point forward to earn its food and its desires only through experiencing more pain and a greater lack of pleasure than all the other creatures. The serpent has caused three kinds of harm by its words: 1) It caused the withdrawal of the glory of God's light which had hovered over Adam and Eve. 2) It resulted in Adam and Eve both becoming mortal, no longer having eternal life. This was the punishment we read about previously (Genesis 2:17) when God told Adam not to eat the fruit of the "tree of the knowledge of good and evil" under penalty of death. This sin was one of disobedience and rebellion. 3) It caused man's limited life on this earth to be a comparatively low-grade quality. Since the serpent made the woman feel as if he had her best interests at heart; and as if his advice to her was motivated by love; God has turned this love into hostility between the serpent offspring and between the woman offspring. Then in verse 16, God pronounced punishment upon Eve. God intended to make it clear that Eve would suffer three curses as retribution for the three features of the tree of knowledge she had wanted to enjoy: 1. She had seen that the tree was good as food; 2. a temptation for the eyes; and 3. desirable to make one knowledgeable. God commanded that instead of enjoying the fruit of the tree, Eve would suffer pains when producing her fruit or children. Regarding the temptation for her eyes Eve wanted to enjoy, God commanded that she would from this point forward have a painful longing for her husband as a passive partner, her husband deciding if to indulge her desire. Finally, instead of satisfying her desire to be God-like, she would be dominated not only by God but also by her husband. God then pronounces the punishment on Adam. One of the first things God said to Adam in verse 17 was **"Because you have heeded the voice of your wife"**. God wanted Adam to know that this was his first sin against Him, accepting the words of his wife without checking them, and because of his failure to investigate his wife's words more closely. He has eaten from the tree. In verse 17-18 **"Cursed *is* the ground for your sake; In toil, you shall eat *of* it All the days of your life. Both thorns and thistles it shall bring forth for you, And you shall eat the herb of the field"**. In this verse God said that instead of Adam being able to plant seeds and it sprouts, the earth will produce thorns and thistles, which are not only useless but will harm the plants that his seed will produce so that he will have to uproot them. God then sent them out of the Garden of Eden. Adam had to leave and go to the place from which he had been created (which was somewhere outside of the Garden of Eden, according to Genesis 2; 7-8); a reference to the earthly part of him, not the divine part of him where he had to perform hard work. There it was a separation between humans and God. After Adam ate of the tree he immediately died spiritually, he was separated from God and he began to die physically. He no longer had eternal life, and he could no longer communicate with God.

CHAPTER FIVE
God's Redemptive Plan

Although there was a separation between humans and God, God had a plan to vanquish sin and Satan one day for all humans. God wants you to have eternal life with Him in heaven. In the book of **Romans Chapter 5 Verses 6-10 NLT** it reads **"When we were utterly helpless, Christ came at just the right time and died for us sinners. Now, most people would not be willing to die for an upright person, though someone might perhaps be willing to die for a person who is especially good. But God showed his great love for us by sending Christ to die for us while we were still sinners. And since we have been made right in God's sight by the blood of Christ, he will certainly save us from God's condemnation. For since our friendship with God was restored by the death of his Son while we were still his enemies, we will certainly be saved through the life of his Son".** God will never stop loving His children, even unto the furthest distance of eternity. You can believe, trust in, or cling to this scripture and become a new creation in Christ Jesus today. Did you know that the moment you believe in Christ as your savior you can be spiritually transformed? This is told to us in the book of **2 Corinthians Chapter 5 Verse 17 NKJV** which reads **"Therefore if anyone is in Christ, he is a new creation; old things have passed away; behold all things have become new".** According to The NKJV study bible, "The term new nature refers to the spiritual transformation that occurs within people when they believe in Christ as Savior." This should cause you to be excited about becoming a child of God and want to spend eternity with God and Jesus in heaven. I know that we have all sinned and deserve God's judgment, but God's grace is the reason we are still here today. In the book of **Ephesians Chapter 2 Verses 8-10 NKJV,** it reads **"For by grace you have been saved through faith, and that not of yourselves; it is the gift of God, not of works, lest anyone should boast. For we are His workmanship, created in Christ Jesus for good works, which God prepared beforehand that we should walk in them"**. What is grace? Grace is unmerited favor or unconditional love. Grace is the love and mercy given to us by God because God desires us to have it, not necessarily because of anything we have done to earn it. It is not a thing, but grace is Jesus, Himself. Grace is favour, the free and undeserved help that God gives us to respond to his call to become children of God, adoptive sons, partakers of the divine nature and of eternal life. Grace means God sending His only Son to descend into hell on the cross so that we guilty ones might be reconciled to God and received into heaven. We read this in **2 Corinthians 5:21 NLT "For God made Christ, who never sinned, to be the offering for our sin, so that we could be made right with God through Christ"**. What does God's grace mean to me? When I think of God's Grace, I think of God's love for me regardless of my imperfections or me feeling undeserving. I want to tell you that this grace is extended to all people, no matter what race, ethnicity, or gender you are. In the book of **Romans Chapter 3, Verses 22-24 NKJV,** it read, **"even the righteousness of God, through faith in Jesus Christ, to all and on all who believe. For there is no difference; for all have sinned and fall short of the glory of God, being justified freely by His grace through the redemption that is in Christ Jesus"**. Now that you have learned all about God's grace for you, I want to tell you you can choose life today by receiving God's grace through Jesus shed blood for you! Jesus can heal the deep sin of your heart and be your friend forever.

CHAPTER SIX
Jesus Is Here

The first sin we read about in chapter 3 has uncovered the root of later sins, but God loves us so much that He sent his son Jesus Christ to be the ultimate sacrifice for all sins. God did this to make a way for us to no longer be separated from Him. In **Romans Chapter 6, Verses 23 NKJV**, it reads **"For the wages of sin is death, but the gift of God is eternal life in Christ Jesus our Lord"**. This scripture means exactly what it says when your life is being controlled by sin there is a price or consequence which is death and being forever separated from God spiritually but, God's gift of salvation to spend eternal life and union with Him because of all Jesus accomplished in His crucifixion (death) to His resurrection (risen) is for you. Jesus lived a perfect, faultless life while He walked the earth, which is why He was the perfect sacrifice. Jesus is the great physician, and His bloodshed on the cross is the cure. Jesus died to purchase our freedom, so you no longer have to be bound by sin. Jesus' purpose was to give us life, and He did just that through His sacrifice. In the book of **John Chapter 10, Verse 10 (NKJV) Jesus said, "The thief (this is the same thief who deceived Eve to eat the fruit) does not come except to steal, and to kill, and to destroy. I have come that they may have life and that they may have *it* more abundantly"**. This abundant life Jesus speaks of includes salvation, freedom, healing, victory, and much more. Jesus was resurrected after His death to save lost people from their sin which Paul expressed in the book of **1 Corinthians Chapter 15 Verses 3-5 NKJV, "For I delivered to you first of all that which I also received: that Christ died for our sins according to the Scriptures, and that He was buried,**

and that He rose again the third day according to the Scriptures, and that He was seen by Cephas, then by the twelve". Jesus' resurrection is relevant because it proves that Jesus has the authority to forgive sin. When Jesus was buried your sins and shame were buried too, now that Jesus has risen sin, death, and hell is conquered and all of your sin and shame is forgiven and left in that empty tomb. This is God's demonstration of His love for us all. Therefore, there should be no room for doubt. You can learn more about Jesus's birth, ministry, death, and resurrection in the first four books of the New Testament part of the bible. I encourage you to read all of those books, Matthew, Mark, Luke, and John. Those books often referred to as the gospels written by four men (Matthew, Mark, Luke, and John) who shared their testament of the life of Jesus. These four men were eyewitnesses to the life and work of Jesus Christ. Notice that each of these men include fine points not exactly matched by the others. That's because each of them saw Jesus Christ from a slightly different angle-the angle known as their perspective. Because God creates each of us as a unique individual, each of us will have a distinct perspective on the events of our lives and the people we encounter in them. These four books are written as a testimony of more than one witness. Each of these stories about the life of Jesus confirms and supports each other. For this reason, we should see the four gospels as a powerful confirmation from God. These books can help you learn how you can follow Jesus as His disciple and by His example.

CHAPTER SEVEN
Receive Christ

Did you know that we are all sinners by nature because of Adam's sin? We read about this in the book of **Romans chapter 5 verse 12-14 "Therefore, just as through one man sin entered the world, and death through sin, and thus death spread to all men, because all sinned — (For until the law sin was in the world, but sin is not imputed when there is no law. Nevertheless, death reigned from Adam to Moses, even over those who had not sinned according to the likeness of the transgression of Adam, who is a type of Him who was to come".** We inherit sin from Adam in our natures in the same way we inherit many of our physical characteristics from our parents. I want you to know that you no longer have to be enslaved to the bondage of sin because Jesus' blood has changed that for each one of us. I want to take this time to invite you to accept Jesus into your heart and life today and all you have to do is **Believe on the Lord Jesus Christ, and you will be saved, you and your household Acts 16; 31 NKJV.** Don't allow the thought of the sins you've committed up to this point stop you from accepting Jesus today. In the book of **John chapter 3 verse 16 NLT, it reads "16 "For this is how God loved the world: He gave his one and only Son (Jesus) so that everyone (you and I) who believes in him will not perish but have eternal life".** Accept Jesus as your Lord and Savior by believing this Good news/Gospel you just read about God sending Jesus, His Son, to die on the cross for all of Our (mines and you're) sins to be forgiven, let us pray,

Lord Jesus, I ask You to forgive my sins and save me from eternal separation from God. I believe that You died for my sins and rose from the dead; I turn from my sins and invite you to come into my heart and life. I want to trust and follow You as my Lord and Savior, please give me the strength, wisdom, and determination to walk in the center of Your will. Satan, I renounce the power and authority I gave you. I take my power and authority back and I give it to Jesus. In Jesus' name, Amen.

My friend, if you just prayed this salvation prayer and believed with all your heart, I want to tell you-you are now a follower of Jesus Christ. God's word tells us that your eternal salvation is secure, In the book of **Romans Chapter 10 verse 9 it reads "that if you confess with your mouth, the Lord Jesus and believe in your heart that God has raised Him from the dead, you will be saved."** You just became a part of God's family, adopted as His very own. In the book of **John Chapter 1 verse 12 NKJV, "But as many as received Him, to them He gave the right to become children of God"**. God can be comparable to your physical father. The word Father meaning is a male parent; a man who has begotten a child, also: a male animal who has sired an offspring. We each have a physical father who gave us life, however, being a father does not always impel something positive. God's word tells us that God is a spirit in **John Chapter 4 Verse 24 NKJV "God is Spirit, and those who worship Him must worship in spirit and truth"**. As we just read God does not have a human body like you and me, He is invisible, He is our spiritual father. God, the Son (Jesus Christ) came to earth in human form but, God, the father did not. God is one in an element and three in person: God the Father, God the Son (Jesus), and the Holy Spirit each person is fully God. Even though God is a spirit, He is also a living, personal being. We can know God personally because of all that Jesus has done. In the book of **1 Peter chapter 3 verse 18 NKJV**, it reads **"For Christ also suffered once for sins, the righteous for the unrighteous, that he might bring us to God, being put to death in the flesh but made alive in the spirit"**. God wants to hear from you each day to stay in communion with you. Your relationship with God is your foundation. What is a foundation? A foundation is a basis (such as a tenet, principle, or axiom) upon which something stands or is supported. As a follower of Christ, your spiritual foundation is crucial to your life, on earth, and in eternity. Following God and submitting to His wisdom empowers you to build a solid foundation based on God's values. As you base your life on Him, there are a few areas you will need to continually focus on cultivating a strong, healthy spiritual life.

1. Have Faith in God- Trust God just as His word tells us in **Isaiah 26: 4 NLT "Trust in the Lord always, for the Lord God is the eternal Rock"**.

2. Family and Godly friendships - hang out with other like-minded people who have a hunger after the things of God, in **Proverbs 12: 26 NLT "The godly give good advice to their friends; the wicked lead them astray"**.

3. Fellowship with other believers - When you fellowship with other believers to worship, pray, or just talk to each other this will help improve your effectiveness just as God's word says in **Proverbs 27:17 NKJV "*As* iron sharpens iron, So a man sharpens the countenance of his friend"**. As you focus on these areas on your walk with God through Jesus, it won't only benefit you, but other people's faith will increase. Now walk it out, be compassionate to everyone that you meet; love, care and be kind to everyone just as Jesus is to you. Don't

forget to go tell someone about your new friend Jesus. I pray that this book has blessed you just as much as it blessed me as I have written it. May God bless you.